SCHUBERT

RONDO IN A MAJOR

OPUS 107; D. 951
FOR ONE PIANO, FOUR HANDS

EDITED BY MAURICE HINSON AND ALLISON NELSON

AN ALFRED MASTERWORK EDITION

Alfred Music Publishing Co., Inc.
P.O. Box 10003
Van Nuys, CA 91410-0003
alfred.com

ISBN-10: 0-7390-8591-3
ISBN-13: 978-0-7390-8591-2

FRANZ SCHUBERT

RONDO IN A MAJOR, OP. 107; D. 951 (FOR ONE PIANO, FOUR HANDS)

Edited by Maurice Hinson and Allison Nelson

Foreword

Franz Schubert (1797–1828) wrote three rondos for piano duet. The first, *Rondo in D Major*, Op. 138; D. 608, was composed early in his career (1818), but published much later (1835). The second, *Rondeau brillant*, Op. 84, No. 2, was composed circa 1825, but not published until 1827. It was meant to be the last movement of a three-movement *Divertissement*, D. 823, for four hands (the other movements being the *Marche brillante*, Op. 63, No. 1, and the *Andantino varié*, Op. 84, No. 1).

The third and final rondo, *Rondo in A Major*, Op. 107; D. 951, is warm and lyrical, having been called "the apotheosis of all Schubert compositions for four hands."[1] It was composed in 1828 for the Viennese company Artaria, which published it shortly after Schubert's death later that year.

ABOUT THE MUSIC

The lyrical themes in the *Rondo* are highly decorative, treated freely, and full of exciting rhythms. Although the dynamic range is limited, exquisite use of p and pp over long periods of time (measures 1–137 for example) create a haunting effect. The writing for both the Primo and Seconcdo is highly effective and equally difficult.

Care should be taken when studying this work. Notice that almost every time a phrase is repeated there is a slight change either in notes or rhythm. In these cases, the fingering must be changed accordingly.

Form: quasi sonata-allegro. **A B A¹ / C / A² B¹ A³**;
the **C** section varies the **B** theme

A = measures 1–68; **B** = 68–102; **A¹** = 102–137;
C = 138–175;
A² = 175–219; **B¹** = 219–241; **A³** = 241–292;
Coda = 292–310.

---

[1] Albert Einstein, *Schubert: A Musical Portrait* (London: Oxford University Press, 1951), 282.

ABOUT THIS EDITION

Ornamentation: Discrepancies between the manuscript and the first edition include some ornamentation being omitted from the latter. The missing ornaments have been restored in this edition.

The *Rondo* uses four types of ornaments. The trill (*tr*) is used six times: in Primo part measures 23, 57, 61, 208, 212, and 309. At the last occurrence, a prefix and termination are added. The turn (∿) is used several times and is always played with the same note pattern. The speed of the turn depends on the length of the note to which it is attached; the longer the main note, the slower the turn. The acciaccatura (♪) and inverted mordent (↞) also appear.

Pedal: The pedal should be used sparingly, and pedaling should be done by the Primo player.

Tempo: The metronome mark is editorial. The work should be fast enough to be energetic, but slow enough to be expressively melodic.

SOURCES CONSULTED

Dale, Kathleen. *Nineteenth-Century Piano Music*. London: Oxford University Press, 1954.

Einstein, Albert. *Schubert: A Musical Portrait*. London: Oxford University Press, 1951.

McGraw, Cameron. *Piano Duet Repertoire*. Bloomington: Indiana University Press, 1981.

Weekley, Dallas and Nancy Arganbright. *Schubert's Music for Piano Four-Hands*. White Plains, NY: Pro/Am Music Resources, Inc., 1990.

Rondo in A Major

SECONDO

Franz Schubert (1797–1828)
Op. 107; D. 951

Rondo in A Major

PRIMO

Franz Schubert (1797–1828)
Op. 107; D. 951

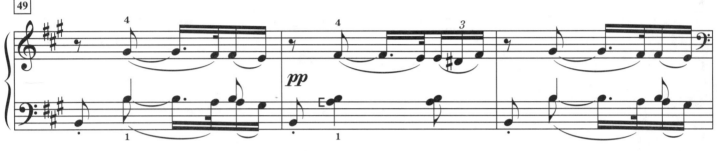

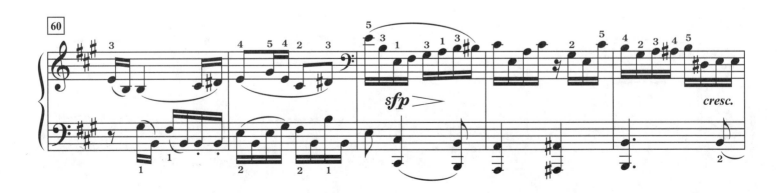

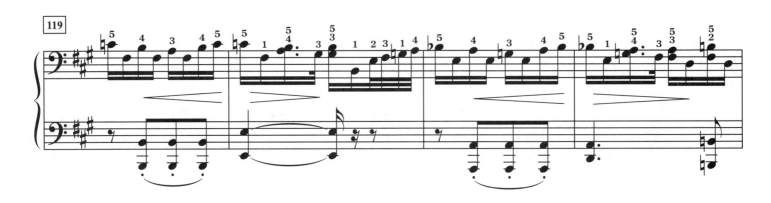

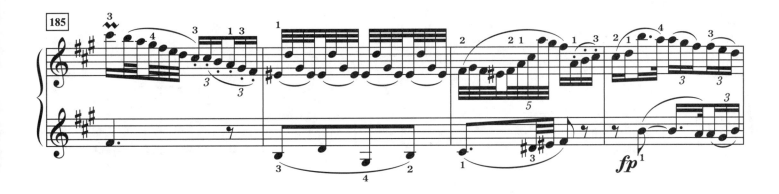

SECONDO

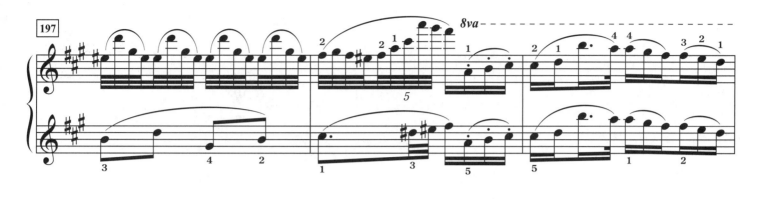

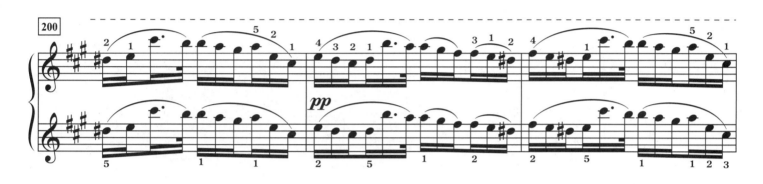

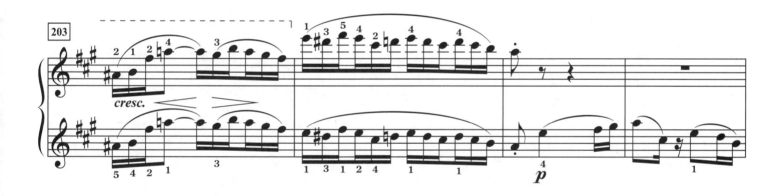

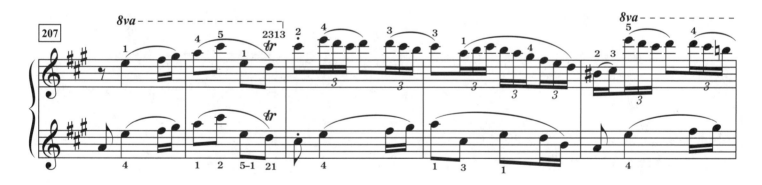

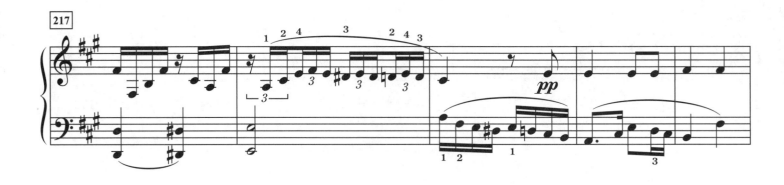

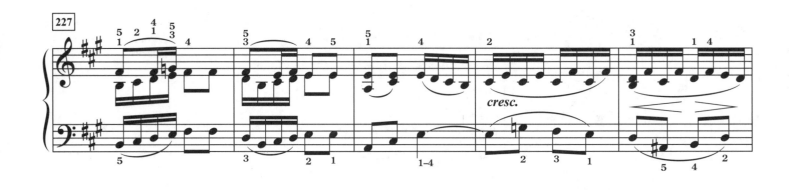

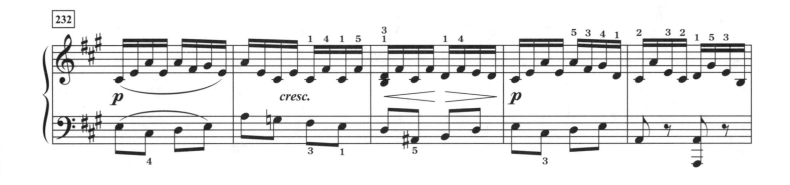

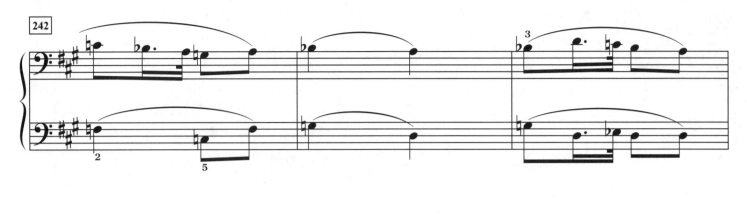

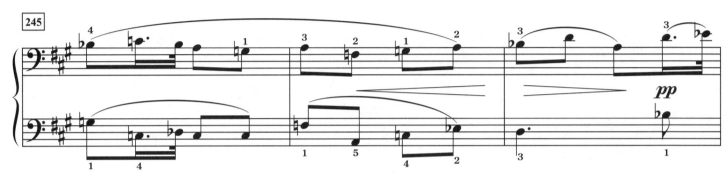

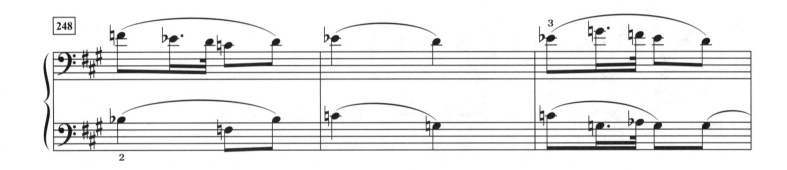

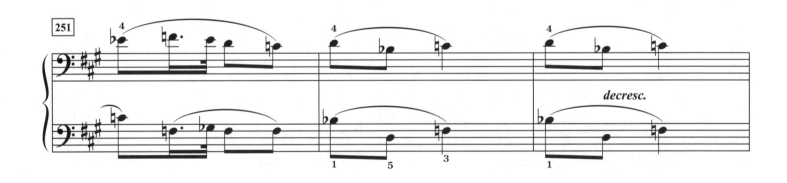

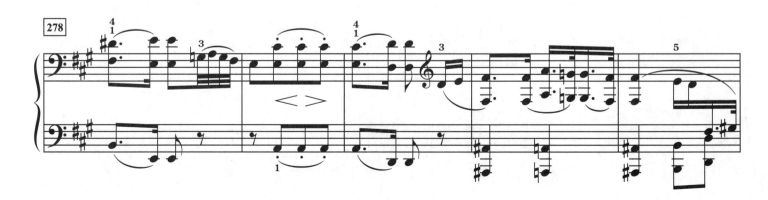